CANADA THROUGH THE DECADES
THE 1990s

Lauri Seidlitz

Weigl
CALGARY
www.weigl.com

Published by Weigl Educational Publishers Limited
6325 - 10 Street SE
Calgary, Alberta, Canada
T2H 2Z9
Web site: http://www.weigl.com
Copyright © 2000 WEIGL EDUCATIONAL PUBLISHERS LIMITED

Canadian Cataloguing in Publication Data

Seidlitz, Lauri, 1966–
The 1990s

(Canada through the decades)
ISBN 1-896990-38-X

1. Canada—History—1963—Juvenile literature.* I. Title. II. Series.
FC635.S45 1999   j971.064'7   C99-910851-4
F1034.2.S34 1999

Printed and bound in Canada
1 2 3 4 5 6 7 8 9 0   03 02 01 00 99

Editor
Leslie Strudwick
Design
Warren Clark
Copy Editors
Rennay Craats
Elizabeth Entrup
Layout
Lucinda Cage

Photograph Credits
Every reasonable effort has been made to trace ownership and to obtain permission to reprint
copyright material. The publishers would be pleased to have any errors or omissions brought to
their attention so that they may be corrected in subsequent printings.

Aboriginal Achievement Awards: page 22B; Archive Photos: pages 10B, 11T-R, 17, 18T, 18B,
19T, 19B, 34B, 35T-L, 35M, 38T, 38B; Jerry Bauer: page 25T; Roberta Bondar: page 26B; Bob
Bosch: page 15T; Boily Photo: page 27; *Calgary Sun*: page 32; Chris Camfield (Michael
Goldman): page 35B-R; *Chatelaine* magazine (Karen Levy): page 43T-L; David Chilton: page
32; Cochran Communications: page 13T; Dan Coleman: page 25B; Corel Corporation: pages 14,
16T, 40B, 41, 42, 43R; CP Picture Archive: pages 11T-L, 11B, 22M, 23T, 34T; Rennay Craats:
page 33; Ego Films (Johnnie Eisen): page 13R; Exploration Products: page 9B; David Fiero:
page 40T; Joel Fournier: page 29B; Geffen Records (Chris Cuffaro): page 35 T-R; Globe Photos:
pages 10T-L, 10T-R; Neil Graham: page 24T; Denise Grant: page 20T; Hibernia Management
and Development Company Ltd.: page 26T; High Cascade Snowboarding Camp: page 34R;
Chuck Kochman: page 32; Andrew MacNaughton: page 24B; Doug MacLellan: pages 30T, 30R,
31T; NBA Canada: page 28B; National Ballet of Canada (Robert Nelson): page 12B-L; Nettwerk
Management: pages 39T (Jay Blakesberg), page 39M (Kharen Hill); Nova Scotia Creative
Services: page 9T; *Ottawa Citizen*: pages 20B, 30L; Photo Run: page 29T; Salter Street Films
(Dan Callis): page 13 B-L; *Saturday Night* magazine: page 43B; Silken & Co.: page 28T;
Starbucks: page 15B; Sullivan Entertainment: page 12B-R; Toni-Lynn Trottier: page 8B; Roger
Turenne: page 8T; Universal Music Group (Derek Shapton): page 39R; *Vancouver Sun*: page 21;
Warner Brothers: page 35B-L; Clyde Warrington: page 12T.

1991

Graham Greene is dancing with celebrity. After his role in *Dances with Wolves*, Greene is nominated for an Academy Award. Page 11 can tell you more.

1991

Yugoslavia is torn apart by civil war and hatred. Turn to page 19 to find out why there is fighting.

1991

Smile—you are on **Operation Desert Storm**. The cameras roll as the Persian Gulf war unfolds before the world's eyes. For more information, go to page 19.

1991

Generation X speaks out through author Douglas Coupland. He publishes his book *Generation X: Tales for an Accelerated Culture* to shed light on just who the Gen Xers are. Who are they? Page 40 has the details.

1992

Westray coal mine is destroyed and reduced to rubble in 1992. Read more about this shocking accident on page 9.

1992

Roberta Bondar is rocketing her way into the history books. What has she done that is so significant? Turn to page 26 to learn more about her accomplishments.

1992

The "Dream Team" is a nightmare to some people. There is still debate over allowing professional athletes to compete in the Olympic Games. For the big picture, turn to page 28.

1992

The Toronto Blue Jays are on top of the world in 1992, then again in 1993. Find out why on page 31.

1992

The English Patient by Canadian writer Michael Ondaatje won literary awards long before his novel became a highly acclaimed movie. For details about the bestseller, see page 25.

1993

Kim Campbell is Canada's "first lady," at least for a little while. But first lady of what? Page 20 will fill in the blanks.

1993

Hockey legend **Mario Lemieux** is faced with the toughest battle of his life. Read more about Canada's favourite Penguin and his off-ice struggle on page 30.

1993

Carol Shields's novel *The Stone Diaries* turns some heads in 1993. She overcame obstacles and finally came out on top. To find out more, turn to page 24.

1994

NHL players are sidelined over contract disputes. How do fans take the break in the action? Tune in to page 30 for the story.

1994

Canadians are invited to take a hike. And millions eagerly await the opportunity. **The Trans-Canada Trail** will link the provinces and territories with recreational trails that will suit anyone's fancy. Find out how this will work on page 31.

Baseball Pros Cleared for 2000 Olympics

Quebec Votes on Sovereignty

Blood Politics

First Female in the NHL

Flood Watch

Nunavut Residents Select New Capital

One Month and Still No Power

Lasagna Unmasked

Teen Dress Is "Crisp" and "Spicy"

Yet even more stories never make the headlines. Every Canadian has a story to tell, with unique experiences and ideas. These personal stories are as much a part of Canada's history as the events the media chooses for the front page. Even the events of your life are a part of Canada's story. If reading this book inspires you to write your own story, which events would you choose as the "headlines?"

You might have many questions after reading this book. How did each event begin? Who was involved? What effects did certain events have on Canadians? What inspired some Canadians to accomplish certain things? You may want to find the answers to some of these questions on your own. If you read a story that interests you, do some research to find out more. Look in encyclopedias and books. Find old newspapers and magazines. Films, CD-ROMs, and the Internet can also be good sources of information.

Introduction

Mordecai Richler Sets off Fury

Grunge Is Out, Jazz Is In

West Coast Fishers at War

Crime on Downward Trend

Fiddlers Dominate East Coast Music Awards

Nisga'a Treaty Called Good Deal by Some

Canada Says "No"

Goodbye Gzowski

Ontario Unions Back Strike

Desert Storm Legacy Full of Clouds

Newspapers are full of headlines. Each headline gives a quick overview of the story underneath. Yet no headline can tell the whole tale. Canada's history is made of millions of stories. But like a newspaper headline, no book can tell Canada's whole tale. *Canada Through the Decades: The 1990s* collects some of Canada's stories during the last ten years of the millennium. Most of the stories in this book made headlines. National newspapers and magazines reported these events, thinking they were important for Canadians to know about and to consider. Learning more about the famous people, events, and trends in the 1990s will help you better understand Canada and Canadians.

Only a few of the stories covered in the media could become part of this book. Some stories were chosen because they were extraordinary, such as the Red River flood in Manitoba. Others were chosen because they were common experiences. People might read these stories and think, "Yes! That is what happened to me!" or "I think that way, too." Both kinds of stories contribute to Canada's history.

Contents

1995

The people of South Africa are free at last. After decades of oppression, **apartheid ends** with the election of their first black president. Who is leading this new nation? Find out on page 18.

1995

The unity of Canada hangs in the balance. Quebec votes on whether to remain a part of Canada or to separate. What did the citizens decide? Page 23 offers some insight.

1995

A medical emergency in Zaire. Africa attracts the attention of the entire world. The effects of the Ebola outbreak can be felt around the globe. Page 18 explains what caused such a panic.

1995

Toronto and Vancouver have something new to fight about. **It is dinosaur pitted against grizzly bear**, providing baskets of fun for Canadian sports fans. Where does this unlikely match-up take place? Turn to page 28 to find out.

1995

Country takes over the cities, at least when **Shania Twain** is leading the charge. She achieves enormous success with her second album. Turn to page 38 to find out how she got where she is.

1996

Nisga'a Nation is given the right to govern its own affairs. Why is this an important development? The answer is found on page 21.

1996

The CFL's plans change, and they settle for the Alouettes. Turn to page 29 to find out what happened.

1997

There is water everywhere! Manitobans bail out of the biggest flood in the province's recent history. There is more about the destructive water on page 8.

1997

A vision of Canadian grace and beauty hangs up her ballet shoes. To find out who retires, see page 12.

1997

Faster than a speeding bullet—maybe not quite that quick, but he is faster than any other human being. To top off his other titles, Donovan Bailey is crowned the world's fastest human. See page 29 for more.

1997

The largest and most expensive oil drilling platform is put in place in 1997. Many people worked hard to get **Hibernia** into the water east of Newfoundland. Find out what is significant about Hibernia on page 26.

1998

If April showers bring May flowers, what do January showers bring? Ontario and Quebec cities are **buried under ice** and left in darkness. For weeks, residents live without water, heat, and electricity after the worst ice storm in history. Turn to page 8 for details.

1998

Canadian writer **Alice Munro** is recognized for *The Love of a Good Woman*. There is more about her on page 25.

1998

CBC and Canadian listeners lose a morning **radio icon**. To learn how Peter Gzowki signed off, turn to page 12.

1999

Céline Dion's heart goes on and on at various 1999 award shows. She won three Grammy Awards in the United States and four Juno Awards in Canada. Most of the awards are for her song "My Heart Will Go On." Find out more about Céline Dion on page 38.

Flood of the Century

Disasters

> **"Cold feet, sore hands, and constantly wet— those are the memories I'll take back,"**

said an officer on his way home from the largest Canadian military operation since the **Korean War**. The 1997 Red River flood was the biggest flood in Manitoba since 1826. Over 8,600 troops and tens of thousands of volunteers dug ditches and piled sandbags to keep back the water.

Land was flooded by the hectare. Thousands of farms, homes, and businesses were destroyed. The flat prairie in the area may be perfect for farming, but it has no natural defenses to stop a flooding river. Once water spreads, it can move for miles. About 28,000 Manitobans were evacuated to safety, leaving thousands of homes under metres of muddy river.

▬ Just before reaching its peak, the Red River's flow reached 3,130 cubic metres per second. This equals 208 dump trucks of water per second!

Ice Storm

Monday, January 5, 1998. Few residents of Ontario and Quebec will forget the heavy rain that began that day. As the rain fell, the water quickly froze, covering everything in sight with inches of ice. Thousands of tree branches fell, taking power lines with them. At the end of the storm, 3 million people were left without electricity, heat, and water. For some, power would not be restored for a month.

"There's nothing of this magnitude in [recorded] history," summed up Stan Siok of the Ottawa weather office.

> **"Weather is always the first and last topic of conversation in Canada. It's because Canadians know painfully well that weather affects our daily lives."**
>
> Mr. Phillips, senior climatologist for Environment Canada

Westray Mine Explosion

A terrible explosion on May 9, 1992, closed the "state-of-the-art" Westray coal mine only eight months after it opened. Twenty-six miners were missing after the explosion rocked Plymouth, Nova Scotia. One hundred ninety-five people risked their own lives in a five-day effort to save the buried workers. Fifteen bodies were eventually recovered, with eleven left **entombed** in the rubble.

Politicians, mine owners, and mine managers were all blamed for the tragedy. Two managers faced criminal charges for ignoring warnings of dangerous conditions from employees. The

▓ The silos at Westray were a reminder of tragedy. In the fall of 1998, the silos were destroyed to ease the pain and to prevent the silos from deteriorating and falling down.

Transportation and Public Works Minister apologized for any role the government may have played in the disaster but no compensation was offered. A report by a Nova Scotia Supreme Court judge called the explosion "predictable and preventable."

Governor General Ray Hnatyshyn later awarded 180 of the rescuers with Medals of Bravery.

SWISSAIR FLIGHT 111

▓ When the emergency call reached Halifax International Airport on September 2, 1998, even the pilot did not know how serious the call really was. Less than thirty minutes later, SwissAir Flight 111 had crashed just a few kilometres off the coast of Nova Scotia.

Witnesses near Peggy's Cove heard a loud bang in the night air. Within two hours, local fishers were at sea hoping to find survivors. Joined by military personnel, the rescue operation battled rough seas and rain as they combed the area. By morning, the reports from the sea were not good. It was clear that all 229 passengers and crew had died in the crash.

The exact cause of the accident remains unknown. In his emergency call, the pilot mentioned smoke in the aircraft. Experts believe an electrical fire may have caused the tragedy.

A Disaster in Waiting?

Residents of British Columbia's lower mainland have been lucky so far. For years, experts have warned people that a large earthquake is a possibility. Disaster planners worry that residents have an "it can't happen here" mindset. They encourage people to prepare emergency kits to help themselves and their families in an earthquake disaster. "The onus comes back to the individual, to the residents to be a little bit more responsible for themselves and to be as self-sufficient as possible," says Heather Lyle, an earthquake planner for the city of Vancouver.

▓ B.C. residents are advised to put together emergency kits in case of an earthquake.

1962 –

Jim Carrey

"All of a sudden, I couldn't understand a word they were saying [at school]. And it made me understand how some kids just can't grasp stuff because of what's going on at home. They're just so full of anger that they can't clue in,"

explained Jim Carrey. Full of anger? The rubber-faced comedian who earns $20 million per movie?

This Canadian-born comedian's life was not always full of laughs. After his father lost his job while Carrey was still in high school, his family became homeless, living for a while in a Volkswagen camper and a tent. He got his start in show business at fifteen as a comedy club ventriloquist. Wearing the polyester suit his mom thought would be a good idea, he was booed off the stage. Now famous for his silliness and facial **distortions**, Carrey has been called a living cartoon.

Titanic Mania

As the nearest port to the *Titanic*'s final resting place, Halifax, Nova Scotia, is forever linked to the 1912 tragedy. Survivors of the accident were taken to New York. The dead were shipped to Halifax, where they were either claimed by relatives or buried. More victims of the *Titanic* are buried in Halifax than in any other city in the world.

More than eighty years later, Canadian director James Cameron and his crew spent seventeen days in Halifax filming a movie about the doomed ship. With renewed interest in the tragedy, Halifax was in the spotlight. Sightseers took *Titanic* tours, leaving flowers and movie tickets on the graves of victims. The grave of James Dawson is the focus of much teenage

Céline Dion had one of her biggest hits with the theme song from the movie *Titanic*, "My Heart Will Go On."

admiration. Historians insisted the young crew member had nothing to do with the **fictitious** Jack Dawson from the movie.

James Cameron made one hit movie after another during the 1990s.

Mountie TV

The image of the Canadian Mountie is the image of a true hero who "always gets his man." Actor, director, and producer Paul Gross brought this image to life in *Due South*, a television show about a Mountie working with the Chicago police force. His handsome, overly polite character has made the program the first Canadian television series to succeed in the tough world of American television. It was watched in a number of countries, with fans exchanging *Due South* trivia on the Internet.

> **"Canadian film and television does not celebrate beauty. In Canada, you can't be serious if you're also attractive."**
>
> Paul Gross, who has lost several acting jobs for being too handsome

TELEVISION

▥ Sets for the television series *Lonesome Dove* were decorated with antiques. A challenge for the show's decorators was making the antiques appear new for the 1870s set. Rick Schroder and Jon Voight starred in the television movie *Return to Lonesome Dove* which, like the series, was filmed in Calgary, Alberta.

Aboriginal Actors Enter Prime Time

Leaving stereotypes from old westerns behind, Canadian actors such as Graham Greene, Tina Keeper, and Tom Jackson have opened doors for Aboriginal actors in film and television. In the 1990 film *Dances with Wolves*, Graham Greene stole scenes from star Kevin Costner. Greene won an Academy Award nomination for his role. He has also won many other awards during his successful career.

▥ *North of 60*'s Tina Keeper won a Gemini Award for best actress in 1997.

It was the television program *North of 60* that really brought Aboriginal communities to Canadian **prime time**. With six successful seasons and 1.5 million loyal viewers, the show had a 90 percent Aboriginal cast, including popular performer Tom Jackson. Sometimes criticized for being too realistic, the series about a small community in the North was a hit in a number of countries.

End of *Morningside*

On May 30, 1998, after 3,000 hours of talk-show programming, Peter Gzowski's CBC Radio show went off the air. For fifteen years, *Morningside* had been a daily ritual for many people. Gzowski interviewed both the famous and not-so-famous. For everyone, Gzowski's program was the place to be heard. It gave an instant career boost to many talented Canadians who might otherwise have gone unnoticed.

Steven Page, lead singer for the Barenaked Ladies, put it this way: "People would come up to us at shows, people of all age groups, grandparents included, and say, 'Oh, I heard you on Gzowski so I had to make the two-hour drive and come see you.' At first, you kind of think, well, geez, *Morningside* is for our parents. But then, as you cross the country, you realize this show is kind of an anchor to remind you that no matter where you are, you're still in Canada."

"With the show ending, the mail has just been overwhelming. It's all very nice, and it's all, 'What are we gonna do without *Morningside*?' But what am I going to do without *Morningside*? This is a really difficult time for me."

Peter Gzowski

Selling Out Avonlea

Canadians watching their country in American films are used to seeing their signs and landmarks disguised. Areas across the country are often made over to appear as American sites in such programs and films as the *X-Files*, *Legends of the Fall*, and *Unforgiven*. Usually, Canadians are tolerant of the changes.

Just do not mess with a Canadian classic. When producers of *Emily of New Moon*, a television show based on the books by L.M. Montgomery, had students in a nineteenth-century classroom say "zee" instead of "zed," they went too far. "They should have 'zed' in there," said an angry language expert from Prince Edward Island, "and if Americans have to scratch their heads, that's too bad." Changes to the book's story to make the show more **contemporary** were also soundly criticized by Montgomery's fans.

DANCE

For twenty-seven years, Karen Kain was one of Canada's favourite ballerinas. She retired from the National Ballet of Canada in 1997 after a cross-country farewell tour.

Sarah Polley starred in *Road to Avonlea*, a series based on characters created by Montgomery.

Tugboat Charm

"My three-year-old son William and I had this running game where we would name all the objects in the house, like the fridge, the couch, the car.

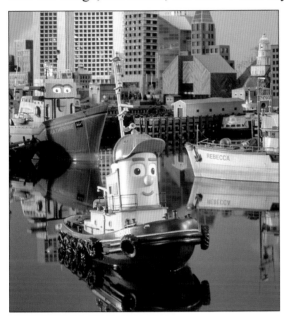

One day while I was down by the harbour, I noticed the tugboats going about their business and in about four minutes I came up with the concept for the show. The name Theodore just popped into my head," explains Andrew Cochrane, producer of the children's television show *Theodore Tugboat*.

Theodore, a fifteen-minute show, has long been an anchor for CBC's morning children's programming. The show features a miniature set of the Halifax harbour, models of real tugboats,

▨ Theodore Tugboat and his cartoon friends delight children with their adventures in the Big Harbour.

"Children's television produced in this country is one of our great secret exports. I think it is a little-known fact that there are literally generations of kids all over the world who are growing up on Canadian children's television shows. "

Andrew Cochrane

and scripts that are often based on real events. This thread of reality keeps the show from being too simple for its young fans.

Watched by children in more than fifty countries, *Theodore* now has an activity web site that draws more than 25,000 visitors a week.

Canadian Jokes and Giggles

What makes Canadians so funny? Jim Carrey, Leslie Nielson, Dan Ackroyd, and Mike Myers are just a few of the famous Canadian comedians of film and television.

Maybe it is because on some nights more people get their news from the television program *This Hour Has 22 Minutes* than from CBC's real news program,

▨ The cast of *This Hour* is from Newfoundland.

The National. This Hour is a **mock** newscast that makes jokes out of the week's real news stories. The show is watched by 1.2 million viewers every week. Cathy Jones, Rick Mercer, Greg Thomey, and Mary Walsh create a group of oddballs that sometimes surprise real politicians for "interviews."

FILM

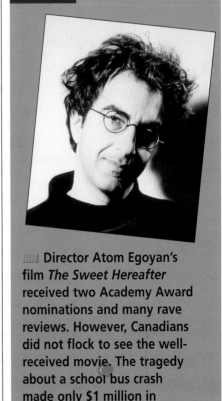

▨ Director Atom Egoyan's film *The Sweet Hereafter* received two Academy Award nominations and many rave reviews. However, Canadians did not flock to see the well-received movie. The tragedy about a school bus crash made only $1 million in Canadian theatres.

On Your Mark!

Get set! Go! And you are off—a proud participant in the **rat race**. Many Canadians complained in the 1990s that they were working too hard. During the decade, hourly wages for educated women fell 12 percent. This means women worked more hours for the same or less money as before. Many people worked seventy to eighty hours a week, leaving little time for family and friends. Carl Costa, a carpet installer, said, "We spend our whole lives chasing dollar bills. It's dollars, money, money." One of Costa's neighbours complained that, "Nobody has time to get to know their neighbours. Isn't that awful?" And it was not just an adult race. Many children were also good rat racers, even in elementary school. Many went to classes, clubs, and sports, with few minutes to spare. Some critics said the young did not even have time to play anymore.

Toward the end of the decade, many people began dropping out of the race. Books on how to simplify your life and relax made the bestseller lists. Working fewer hours, spending less money, and making more time for family were common goals for people adapting to a simpler lifestyle.

▥ Canadians have grown tired of racing through life. People have started to choose relaxation over the rat race.

Cirque du Soleil

In 1987, Guy Laliberte decided to take the Cirque du Soleil to the Los Angeles Festival. It was a make-or-break gig for his young company. The Cirque was formed by a group of street performers in 1984. "We went down there

> **"We never forget where we come from and we come from the street. Our shows have no age barrier, no class barrier. When Vegas was looking for family entertainment, they called the Cirque; when Disney wanted adult entertainment in Orlando, they called the Cirque."**
>
> Daniel Gauthier, president of Cirque du Soleil

barely paying for the gasoline," he remembered. "The festival had no advance money. So I said, 'I'll take the risk, but give me some publicity and the opening-night slot.' It was a hit. The next day, the scalpers were making money from us. But if we had failed, we had no money to bring our equipment back to Quebec."

In the 1990s, the Montreal-based company was a huge success. Each performance mixed dance, music, theatre, and acrobatics. The company has won more than seventy awards for art and business and has sold more than 17 million tickets to its performances around the world.

Slang

da bomb
good; very good; the best

like
no meaning—a filler

'sup?
What's up—a greeting

fly
to leave; cool

chill
to relax

phat
good; cool; great; awesome

stoked
very happy; excited

dis
to show disrespect

Bumps and Bruises

Wrist fractures, sprained fingers, muscle pulls, and bruises. Hospitals saw these injuries rise during the 1990s. The cause was often inline skating. Canadian hospitals reported thirty-three inline skating injuries in 1991 and almost 900 in 1995. From 1989 to 1999, 4 million pairs of inline skates were sold in Canada. Doctors wanted to see more safety equipment sold along with the skates. Doctors said helmets and wrist, knee, and elbow guards should be worn by beginners and experienced skaters alike. People wearing safety gear accounted for only 7 percent of injuries.

▨ Roller hockey leagues sprouted up all across Canada due to the popularity of inline skates.

Spin-off activities were also popular. By 1998, Toronto had over fifteen roller hockey leagues, with around 200 players in each league. Inline skating arenas sprang up across the country. Races were popular as well. The winner of a 42-kilometre race in Ottawa averaged 30.5 kilometres per hour. For many young inline skaters, tricks were the name of the game. Some rode ramps and did tricks on rails, often in special inline skating parks. "It's such a thrill. It becomes your life," said one inline skating competitor.

Millennium Plans

Many people in Canada are spending 1999 preparing for New Year's Eve. January 1, 2000, will be celebrated as the first day of a new millennium. For people with a great deal of money, the celebration choices are endless. Some people will pay $150,000 each to attend a party in Cancun, Mexico. Others will pay $1,000 per ticket to attend a five-day concert and party in the California desert. Others will take a cruise to the **International Date Line**, trying to be among the first on the planet to greet the new year. Some hotels in cities such as New York and Las Vegas have been booked for years.

Yet other people are making different plans. They are more worried than excited about the year 2000. These people fear the "millennium bug." This bug is sometimes called the Y2K problem. Y2K stands for Year 2000. It is a problem that may affect many computers around the world. Some computers may not recognize the year 2000 and might think it is the year 1900. This could cause serious problems in services such as banking. Some people are preparing for the new year by stocking food and water in case there are problems. They worry that grocery stores may not receive regular food shipments. So many businesses and services depend on computers that it is hard to predict what might happen. Even computer experts do not know for sure.

COFFEE

▨ Java. Latte. Cappuccino. Decaf. Cuppa Joe. Canadians were crazed for coffee in the 1990s. Coffee shops appeared in neighbourhoods across the country and became a popular meeting place.

End of an Empire

"I have **relinquished** the **administration** of this government. God save the queen." With these words, Hong Kong's last governor, Chris Patten, closed a chapter in the history of Hong Kong In July 1997, Great Britain returned Hong Kong to Chinese control, ending their ninety-nine-year lease of the territory.

For some, the event was nothing special. "Who cares about the end of an empire? I came here because there's lots of money to be made," said a British construction worker. For people worried about Hong Kong's **democratic** traditions,

More than 5 million people live in Hong Kong.

the switch to Chinese control was a concern. Just six hours after British troops left, Chinese tanks and troops arrived to take their place.

Death of the People's Princess

The August 1997 accident shocked the world. Princess Diana had died in a car speeding through a tunnel in Paris. The car's chauffeur lost control at a speed of about 160 kilometres/hour, sending the Mercedes crashing into a pillar. The driver, Diana, and her friend, Dodi Fayed, were all killed.

Blame and anger for the accident were put on the photographers pursuing the car. Anger turned to shock when people discovered that the photographers at the scene had shot photos of the dying princess. In the end, all feelings turned to sympathy for Diana's two sons, William and Harry.

Tigers in Trouble

In the 1980s, countries in Southeast Asia were called tigers because of their quick **economic** growth. By 1998, everything had changed. In one year, the value of Asian monies had fallen greatly: 50 percent in the Philippines, 61 percent in Malaysia, and 377 percent in Indonesia. A Hong Kong apartment that sold for $1 million in 1997 was worth half the price in 1998. Hardworking professionals sold hats and scarves on the street, trying to earn a living any way they could.

The economy in Asia is not expected to get much better in the near future. In some areas, recovery and growth are not predicted to occur until 2005. Until then, citizens in Asian countries are left to cope with unemployment and fear.

As poverty spread through the densely populated countries, the number of people with nothing to lose grew rapidly. Many feared this explosive situation. In November 1998, Indonesian students led riots against their army and government. In one night, more than fourteen people died and over 200 were injured as soldiers shot at protesters with rubber bullets. Most observers said the riots were only the

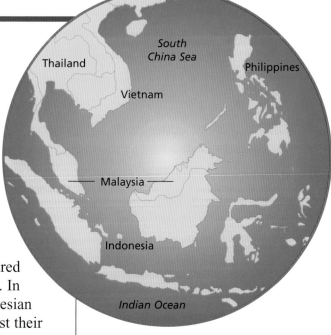

beginning of a bloody **revolution**. Other nations in the region watched Indonesia's problems with growing fear for their own futures.

Moving Past the Troubles

"The Troubles" officially began in Londonderry, Ireland, on Bloody Sunday. On that day in 1972, thirteen people were killed by British soldiers trying to control a demonstration. During the next three decades, Protestants fought Catholics, terrorists fought soldiers, and neighbours fought neighbours. Londonderry was a war zone.

▬▬ Peace talks continued through 1999, but the Troubles are still not over or forgotten.

By 1998, a new mood had taken hold of the country. People were worn down by violence and saw no military victory in sight. Seventy-one percent of the population voted in favour of a peace agreement. People were ready to help their country move past the fighting. A Protestant politician noted that it would take time to recover from the years of bitterness. "Remember, you have nearly three generations of people in this country who have gone through a war with their neighbours as the enemy."

Rwandan Genocide

It has been called one of the greatest crimes against humanity since the **Holocaust** in Nazi Germany. On April 4, 1994, Hutu extremists began a plan in which 800,000 Tutsis were killed in 100 days. That equals 8,000 people killed a day, a third of whom were children.

Canadian General Romeo Dallaire had been in charge of the small United Nations peacekeeping force in the country since 1993. He had been told the mission was going to be easy. His 2,600 troops were poorly trained and lacked equipment. Nobody even gave Dallaire

▬▬ The Hutu and Tutsi are two different **ethnic** groups. Both groups came to the Rwandan region centuries ago from other parts of Africa.

a map of the country—he had to go out and buy one. How wrong they all were. Missing one opportunity after another to stop the killings, the United Nations failed Rwandans and the international community.

> "There are international early warning systems that automatically trigger world response in the case of famines, medical epidemics, and nuclear disasters. Rwanda surely suggests that at last it is time to treat the mass slaughter of whole populations with equal urgency."
>
> Brian Stewart, CBC correspondent

Outbreak Alert

World health authorities went on high alert in May 1995. Reports of a deadly virus in Zaire sent health officials rushing to the African country. The Ebola virus kills 80 percent of the people it contacts within days. Of the 144 cases in Zaire, 121 of the victims died. Concerned countries **quarantined** anyone who might have been in contact with the disease.

Many feared the Ebola virus was a sign of the future. New diseases may spread more rapidly than ever before in human history because of advances in transportation. Even the flu had doctors concerned. Some health authorities predicted a worldwide flu epidemic that could kill millions of people. The 1918–1919 epidemic killed 50,000 Canadians and over 20 million others around the world. People feared the next outbreak could be worse.

■■■ **Medics worked quickly to contain the Ebola virus, often covering themselves to avoid contamination.**

End of Apartheid

In 1995, after one year as South Africa's first black president, Nelson Mandela said, "We have achieved far beyond what we expected. In twelve months, we have gone a long way to changing some of the evils that have haunted the majority of people in this country for the past 300 years." These evils included a system of **apartheid,** which kept the black majority as unequal citizens in their own country.

■■■ **Many blacks in South Africa were impatient for change. One man asked in 1995, "Are we in power or simply in government? Ordinary people like me have not experienced any change."**

After twenty-seven years in prison, Nelson Mandela was released in 1990. Mandela had been in jail since 1963 for his political activities. His release and the lifting of the ban on his political party, the African National Congress, marked the beginning of a new era for the country.

Operation Desert Storm

An officer in the American army compared the Gulf War to a football game in which "only our team showed. We had the only ball, too." When the Iraqi army under Saddam Hussein's command invaded Kuwait on August 2, 1990, the **allied** response launched a new era in warfare.

In early 1991, nearly two dozen allied countries, including the United States and the former Soviet Union, launched Operation Desert Storm. In forty days of air attacks and less than one hundred hours of ground fighting, the Iraqi army retreated. Baghdad, the capital of Iraq, had lost communication, electricity, water, and sewage services. Only 148 allied soldiers lost their lives, compared to 200,000 Iraqis. Critics of the campaign said more civilians lost their lives than were made public. They charged that sanctions against Iraq continued to make people suffer.

▩ The Gulf War launched CNN as an international site for news. Even soldiers in Saudi Arabia turned to the network to catch news of the war they were fighting.

All the King's Men

Nobody could put Yugoslavia back together again. In June 1991, Slovenia and Croatia declared their **independence** from the Yugoslavian federation of republics. The following month, Serbian armies began forcing people out of Serbian territory, claiming to be doing so in an attempt to protect their land. Millions of people were driven from their homes. Many people were beaten, tortured, and even killed. Croatians and Muslims fought back with violent acts of their own.

By October, ethnic hatred going back hundreds of years had exploded into civil war. The Serbian-dominated Yugoslav army fought first Slovenia, then Croatia.

When Bosnia declared its independence in 1992, United Nations troops were sent into the region to stop the civil war. Once the proud host of the winter Olympics, the city of Sarajevo had snipers trading bullets across rubble-filled streets. Peace agreements in 1997 and 1999 gave temporary hope, but fighting continued to erupt.

▩ The former Yugoslavia has been left in ruins and millions of people have to start over again.

1948 – POLITICIAN AND LAWYER

Kim Campbell

Rising from Vancouver School Board member to the position of prime minister in just twelve years, Kim Campbell was clearly smart and ambitious. The woman who was Canada's first female prime minister was not afraid to make fun of herself. When a fun photo of Campbell holding her judicial robes out in front of her bare shoulders was published in a book of famous Canadians, a fellow member of Parliament called her the "Madonna of Politics."

Her six-month reign as government leader ended when the Progressive Conservative party lost the 1993 election to the Liberals. Although some held Campbell partly responsible for the loss, many others saw her as only one part of a party that had become unpopular.

Charlottetown Accord

On October 26, 1992, Canadians were asked to approve a set of constitutional changes written by four Aboriginal organizations, the two territorial governments, and all the provincial governments except Quebec. Their response? A clear "No" that quashed attempts to revise the constitution for the rest of the decade. The **referendum** failed in six provinces and by an overall majority of Canadians, 54.2 percent to 44 percent. Many voters explained their choice by saying the accord was too vague about too many important points.

Tainted Blood: Scandal and Responsibility

"I want people to own up to what happened," stated Christian Pelletier, twenty-year-old victim of tainted blood. "I really need someone to say 'I'm sorry,'" echoed Sue McCutcheon, whose husband died after receiving bad blood during open-heart surgery.

In the 1980s, thousands of people received blood during medical treatments that made them sick with diseases such as AIDS and Hepatitis C. Politicians, Red Cross officials, and members of the medical community all had a part in failing to protect sick people from bad blood products. A 1,138-page report on the scandal stated that even minimal safety precautions would have prevented the tragedy.

People who received tainted blood between 1986 and 1990, around 6,600 across the country, were **compensated** by the government. These years were chosen because blood screening could have been in place but was not.

On October 10, 1998, forty-five-year-old Kim Rowe put up 7,000 white crosses on the lawn of Parliament Hill to represent the number of people who will eventually die from tainted blood. "I'm hoping Canadians will look at this sculpture and say, 'Why did this have to happen?'"

The New North, Strong and Free

On April 1, 1999, **cartographers** redrew the map of Canada for the first time since 1949 when Newfoundland joined Confederation. On that day, the Northwest Territories divided, and the eastern territory became Nunavut. Until this point, the region was isolated from the rest of Canada. Goo Arlooktoo, a political leader from the region, was fourteen years old when he saw his first tree on a student exchange trip to Montreal. Where he grew up, there were no televisions or magazines. Few people in his community spoke English.

Much of this situation changed during the 1990s. Although most residents lived a traditional Inuit lifestyle, multi-channel television made them more aware of life in the South. "When we got other channels besides the CBC, professional wrestling became a really big thing. I mean really big. Hunters would rush home at the end of the day to watch the 6 o'clock fights," explained Arlooktoo.

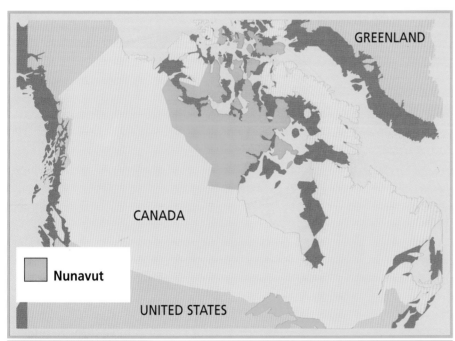

Nunavut

CANADA

GREENLAND

UNITED STATES

Nunavut Facts

- Eighty-three percent of Nunavut's population is Inuit.
- *Nunavut* means "our land" in Inuktitut.
- The entire territory has a population of 24,665.
- The territory covers 2.2 million square kilometres. This is twice the size of Ontario.
- Nunavut crosses three time zones.
- Forty percent of Nunavut's population is under fifteen years old.
- The capital is Iqaluit, which used to be called Frobisher Bay.

Nisga'a Nation

There are about 6,000 Nisga'a members living in the Nass Valley and throughout the province of British Columbia.

"The journey our forefathers began well over a century ago ended this morning," said Joseph Gosnell, president of the Nisga'a Tribal Council. The agreement, announced in February 1996, was the first land claims treaty in British Columbia's history. It gave the Nisga'a peoples a list of rights that many other Aboriginal groups can only call distant goals. The treaty was officially approved in July 1998.

The Nisga'a had their own constitution, government, and police force, giving them the ability to run their own affairs. The agreement also settled claims for the area's resources, such as fish and forests. Yet the treaty's importance went beyond resources. "It's not just a question of land and money, it's [an] obligation to the First Nations of the province," said one B.C. Supreme Court judge.

Preston Manning

When your father was premier of Alberta for twenty-five years and then a Canadian senator for another thirteen, you cannot avoid his influence. Preston Manning based his political career on lessons from his father, Ernest Manning: "The salt of the earth are the smallest potatoes." Taking this advice, Manning based his party on support from

"Canada has got problems but we've got the resources to cope with them."

Preston Manning

ordinary Canadians. The Reform party grew quickly since its beginning. It started with 3,000 members at the 1987 founding convention in Vancouver. Within ten years, it moved into the position of **Official Opposition.**

Oka Stand-off

The Mohawk residents of the Kanesatake reserve in Quebec decided they could not stand by and let a golf course expand onto land they considered sacred. Instead, they blockaded a bridge. What began as a protest in the summer of 1990 grew. For seventy-eight days, people across Canada and around the world watched a real-life drama play out before them. Television viewers saw Quebec residents shout and throw stones at cars of seniors, women, and children moving in and out of the reserve.

▦ The Oka stand-off lasted for seventy-eight days.

"They [the government] knew we have to be involved as Aboriginal people in places like the legislature and parliament, where decisions are made, when laws are made. It took me ten days just to say one word."

Elijah Harper on the Meech Lake Accord

Anger grew. Guns, threats, and masked **defiance** marked the showdown involving members of the Mohawk nation, the Quebec provincial police, and finally the Canadian army.

Ronald Cross, who became known as the masked warrior "Lasagna," explained his decision to join the protest: "I got mad. I saw all the police and all the guns and I decided that I was going to do something to stop my people from being pushed around."

Quebec Referendum

"Whatever happens, I'll be able to say I tried to do something when the chips were down." The words of this young Newfoundlander on his way to a unity rally in downtown Montreal expressed the feelings of many other Canadians who made the rally a success. Tens of thousands hit Montreal's streets just three days before the 1995 Quebec referendum on **sovereignty**.

Although separatists said the rally would not affect the vote, the question was defeated on October 30, 1995. However, the results were too close for either side to claim a clear victory. Those voting "No" to separation were 50.6 percent. The other 49.4 percent voted "Yes." Canadians watching the votes come in were on the edge of their seats all night.

A year after the referendum, a Quebec pollster insisted that, "Quebeckers are waiting. Basically waiting for the federal government to offer Quebec something substantial. It's clear in the polls that the Quebec population wants to stay in Canada, but not just any Canada, or at any price. That's the key."

"The day of the rally I was sort of down like most people were I think.... I turned onto Peel Street and there was a sea of flags. It was as far as you could see. It was flags waving and people laughing and it was an incredible sight."

Terry Tamelti

MILITARY

▓ When Barry and Jennifer Armstrong exposed the murder of two teenagers by members of the Canadian military while in Somalia, their lives changed forever. The March 4, 1993, killing shocked the Canadian public. Although many criticized the army doctor and his wife for their actions, others applauded them.

Constitutional Time Line

May 21, 1990

Lucien Bouchard forms the Bloc Québécois, a federal political party supporting Quebec separation.

June 13, 1990

Meech Lake Accord fails in Manitoba and Newfoundland.

November 1, 1990

Brian Mulroney asks Canadians to discuss their visions for Canadian unity.

June 27, 1991

Citizens' Forum on National Unity gives its report.

August 28, 1992

Charlottetown Accord signed. Defeated two months later in a national referendum.

October 25, 1993

Conservatives beaten in landslide Liberal party victory.

October 30, 1995

Quebeckers defeat sovereignty question.

January 26, 1996

Bouchard leaves federal politics and becomes leader of the Parti Québécois and premier of Quebec.

September 14, 1997

Calgary Declaration asks for public opinion on how to recognize Quebec's unique status within Canada.

August 20, 1998

The Supreme Court of Canada rules that Quebec cannot leave Canada without negotiations, no matter what happens in a provincial referendum.

1935 –

Carol Shields

The Stone Diaries

Carol Shields faced more bad reviews than good reviews in her early career. When she began her master's degree at the University of Ottawa in 1965, she was one of the few married women with children in the program. The university had not wanted her to join the course, but they finally allowed her to begin. Years later, reviews of her first books were not promising. A reviewer in *Maclean's* magazine called Shields's first novel "smaller than life."

As Shields continued to publish, however, more people praised her work. Then in 1993, when she published *The Stone Diaries,* the praise would not stop. *The Stone Diaries* tells the story of a woman's life over eighty years. Among other honours, the book

"I guess I'm just interested in how people tell their life stories, or if it's even possible to tell your life story."

Carol Shields

won a Governor General's Award in Canada and the Pulitzer Prize in the United States. At almost sixty years of age, Carol Shields had become an international publishing success.

TRUE CRIME

Author Margaret Atwood did not disappoint her fans with her 1996 release, *Alias Grace*. The novel is based on a true story of murder and scandal. In 1843, sixteen-year-old Grace Marks was accused of murdering her employer and his housekeeper. Atwood's book tells her own version of Grace's story.

Governor General's Award Winners for Children's Literature (Text)

1990
Redwork
by Michael Bedard
La Vrai Histoire du chien de Clara Vic
by Christiane Duchesne

1991
Pick-Up Sticks
by Sarah Ellis
Deux heures et demie avant Jasmine
by François Gravel

1992
Hero of Lesser Causes
by Julie Johnston
Victor
by Christiane Duchesne

1993
Some of the Kinder Planets
by Tim Wynne-Jones
La Route de Chlifa
by Michelle Marineau

1994
Adam and Eve and Pinch-Me
by Julie Johnston
Une belle journée pour mourir
by Suzanne Martel

1995
The Maestro
by Tim Wynne-Jones
Comme une peau de chagrin
by Sonia Sarfati

1996
Ghost Train
by Paul Yee
Noémie-Le Secret de Madame Lumbago
by Gilles Tibo

1997
Awake and Dreaming
by Kit Pearson
Pien
by Michel Noël

1998
The Hollow Tree
by Janet Lunn
Variations sur un même & Lagno, T'aime
by Angèle Delaunois

The Love of Alice Munro

Writer Alice Munro has often received praise for her writing. During the last three decades she wrote short story collections, articles, and a novel. She was short-listed for the Booker Prize, and she has come away with one of Canada's highest literary awards, the Governor General's Award for fiction, three times. Munro also won the Canadian Booksellers Association International Book Year Award and the PEN/Malamud Award for Excellence in Short Fiction, among others. In 1998, she added to that list by winning the Giller Prize for literature for her collection of short stories entitled *The Love of a Good Woman*. This book explores what people will do, both good and bad, for love.

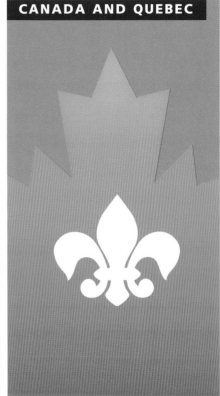

▓ Quebec politicians and newspapers were in an uproar in 1992. The cause? Mordecai Richler's new book, *Oh Canada! Oh Quebec! Requiem for a Divided Country.* Richler was no stranger to controversy. His books and articles often provoked people. *Oh Canada! Oh Quebec!* was no different. It criticized Quebec separatists and accused them of being **prejudiced** against Jewish people.

The separatists were not the only people criticized. Richler wrote that people in the rest of Canada were prejudiced as well. His book also questioned why Canada was always on the brink of breaking up. In *Oh Canada! Oh Quebec!*, Richler asked why the French and English could not "learn to celebrate what binds them together."

1943 –

Michael Ondaatje

The English Patient

"*The English Patient* began with a vision: a burning man in the desert," said author Michael Ondaatje. The novel tells the story of a Canadian nurse in World War II who is caring for a dying patient in Italy. The patient tells a love story that captivates the nurse. Most of *The English Patient*'s readers were also captivated. The book won the 1992 Governor General's Award for fiction and shared the Booker Prize in Britain. It was the first time a

Canadian had won the important British award. The novel was later made into an Academy Award-winning film.

The Hibernia Oil Field

Called the ninth wonder of the modern world by *Time* magazine, the Hibernia platform was towed into place in June, 1997. It sits 315 kilometres southeast of Newfoundland in the stormy waters below Iceberg Alley. In these difficult conditions, Hibernia, owned by a group of oil companies and the federal government, began producing from the only platform designed to withstand the impact of a 1 million tonne iceberg.

Building one of the heaviest structures ever moved on Earth was no small task. Even building the construction site cost $1 billion. Two mountains were levelled and a lake was drained to make room for the project. To ease environmental concerns, all the fish in the lake were moved to a neighbouring lake before the water was drained.

Six years after construction began, the Hibernia oil field went into production in November 1997—the platform was the first of its kind in the world. At 40,000 barrels of oil per day, Hibernia's first well set a Canadian record for crude oil production. In 1999, it stands as the fifth largest oil field in Canada.

> "We developed the concept of the 10,000-year iceberg. In other words, we tried to predict the biggest iceberg that could have a chance of arriving in 10,000 years. And we designed [Hibernia] to withstand that."
>
> Francois Sedillot, design engineer on the project

Measuring Hibernia

- The entire Hibernia platform weighs 1.2 million tonnes.
- At 224 metres, it is about the height of the Calgary Tower.
- It contains enough reinforcing steel to build fifteen Eiffel Towers.

1945 – ASTRONAUT AND SCIENTIST

Roberta Bondar

"Yes, Yes, Yes." Fists in the air, Roberta Bondar chanted to the watching crowd as she walked toward the space shuttle *Discovery*. Nine years after beginning her training, Bondar finally made Canadian history on January 22, 1992. She became the second Canadian and first Canadian woman in space.

> "As human beings on the surface we have a very short-term [idea] of survival—we need to think more about the survival of the planet as a whole. We're so small we think the horizon goes on forever. When you're in space, you realize it doesn't."
>
> Roberta Bondar

GROWTH OF THE INTERNET

One of the biggest changes during the 1990s was the worldwide growth of Internet users. Developed in the 1960s as a communications network for military officials, Internet use exploded during the last decade. At the end of the decade, it was estimated that a new person logged on to the Internet every 1.6 seconds!

**1975 –
FOUNDER OF INTERLOG
INTERNET SERVICES**

Matt Harrop

His staff had a good laugh the day Harrop was turned down for a credit card from his bank. Even though **investors** were offering to buy his two-year-old company for $4 million, he was not considered a good credit risk. As a Canadian business magazine stated: "[Harrop] looks more like the guitarist for the punk-pop band Green Day than an entrepreneurial wunderkind."

After dropping out of high school, Harrop used a small loan to build what is now a major player in the Internet service industry. Although Harrop himself was an unusual businessperson, his success story was not. Harrop saw an opportunity, took a chance, and worked eighteen-hour days to make his dream come true.

Confederation Bridge

Opened for traffic on May 31, 1997, the 12.9-kilometre Confederation Bridge joined Prince Edward Island to New Brunswick. It allowed travel to the island twenty-four hours a day. It was the longest bridge over ice-covered waters in the world. At the water level, the bridge was designed like an ice-breaker. When ice hits, "The ice always loses and the bridge always wins," stated one bridge official.

▨ Many of the huge pieces for the bridge were built on land and lifted into place by a crane that stood thirty-five storeys off the water surface.

Where have the cod gone?

Fishers, scientists, and politicians were left scratching their heads as cod stocks dropped from somewhere in the million-tonne range in 1990 to around 20,000 tonnes by mid-decade. A ban on cod fishing did not bring them back, either. Reasons for the disappearing fish ranged from overfishing, water temperature

> **"It's [possible] that treating the atmosphere as the world's largest garbage dump is already having an impact on the environment."**
>
> Louise Comeau, Sierra Club

changes, a shortage of food, and a larger seal population. Some scientists warned that turbot stocks and British Columbia salmon might be next to decline.

> "I believe in fair play. I believe in personal excellence and achievement of goals through fair means. And I think this is where this decision made today hurts me the most."
>
> Silken Laumann at a press conference after losing her medal

Keeping Gold

Can Canada keep its gold medals? For many Canadians, the announcement that snowboarder Ross Rebagliati had failed his drug test and would lose his gold medal sounded all too familiar. Rebagliati won gold at the 1998 Winter Olympics in Nagano, Japan. It was the first time snowboarding was an official Olympic sport. Although he fought the decision and won back his medal a few days later, Canadians had mixed reactions to the controversy. For many, Rebagliati's argument that he had not used drugs recently was still a national embarrassment.

Some remembered their disappointment when rower Silken Laumann failed a drug test and lost her gold medal at the 1995 Pan American games. Canadians sympathized when they found out her failed test was due to a doctor's mistake and a cold medicine that contained a banned drug. Laumann had become a national hero in 1992 when she recovered from a serious rowing accident to win a bronze medal at the Barcelona Olympics. Remembering the international scandal when sprinter Ben Johnson lost his Olympic gold medal in 1988, Canadians were concerned about the tarnished reputation of their athletes.

Olympic Medals Over the Decade

	Gold	Silver	Bronze	
1992	7	4	7	= 18
1994	3	6	4	= 13
1996	3	11	8	= 22
1998	6	3	4	= 13

The 2000 Olympics in Sydney will see professional baseball players as part of its competition. By voting to change its amateurs-only rule, the International Baseball Association followed in the footsteps of basketball, hockey, skating, tennis, and cycling. Barcelona's 1992 games were the first to include professional athletes. The American "Dream Team" has dominated basketball at the Olympics ever since.

Critics said professional participation went against the spirit of the Olympic Games. International competition among hard-working amateur athletes should be the focus, not millionaires gathering to dominate their sport. Many fans seemed to agree. A poll by the American sports network ESPN found that 59 percent of people surveyed said they rooted for the underdog in games against basketball's dream team.

BASKETBALL

With the Raptors and the Grizzlies, Toronto and Vancouver became the first cities outside the United States to join the National Basketball League during the 1995–96 season.

Jacques Villeneuve Takes the Prize

"**I** had to go for it, even if I ended up in the dirt," Villeneuve said, explaining his daring move to reporters. He drove up next to his rival, Michael Schumacher, on the inside lane. Schumacher swerved, hit the back end of Villeneuve's car and crashed off the track. Villeneuve flew past to become the first Canadian to win the 1997 Formula One world driving championship.

Sometimes criticized for being too reckless, Villeneuve maintained that, "When you are inside the race car, you believe you control the situation. You have 100 percent confidence in yourself, so you don't think of getting killed." Jacques's father, Gilles, was one of the most famous Formula One drivers in the world. Gilles Villeneuve died in a crash when Jacques was eleven years old.

Formula One Facts

- It costs well over $10 million a year to equip Jacques Villeneuve and his team.

- One car may go through a dozen sets of tires every racing season. Back tires cost $1,700.00 each and front tires cost $1,200.00.

- New engines cost $140,000.00. Each engine has to be rebuilt after 500 miles.

- Formula One cars can reach speeds of up to 240 kilometres/hour.

- More than 160,000 fans attend the Toronto and Vancouver Indy events.

"I support my teammates and they support me and we're successful.... If we can do it through sport, I don't see why we can't do it as a country."
Donovan Bailey

The World's Fastest Human

It seemed at first like the simplest contest possible. Two men ran 150 metres to see who would win. But when the men were sprinters Donovan Bailey and Michael Johnson, the contest became a major sporting event watched around the world. The two athletes had developed a public rivalry. Sports fans in over fifty countries tuned into the race in June 1997.

In a few seconds, it was over. Canadian Donovan Bailey won the race and claimed the title as the world's fastest human.

Adding the win to his 1996 Olympic gold medals in the 100-metre race and 4 x 100-metre relay, Bailey's future looks bright. He has set his sights on a gold medal at the 2000 Olympic Games in Sydney, Australia.

FOOTBALL

In 1996, efforts to expand the Canadian Football League into the United States died. After a nine-year absence, football returned to Montreal. Disbanded earlier, the Alouettes are a new team in 1996.

Canada's Sport in Trouble

It was about greed, not goals. At least that is how some fans began to see Canada's favourite sport. Hockey turned into big business. In 1990, the average NHL salary was $200,000 U.S. By 1998, the average was well over $1.1 million U.S. It was little wonder that fans had trouble understanding player demands during the 1994 NHL lockout.

Canadian teams could not compete with player salaries. Four of the six Canadian NHL teams in the twenty-six-team league sometimes worried more about survival than about strategies for the next game. Since 1996, two NHL teams left Canada for the United States. Quebec City lost its Nordiques to Colorado, and the Jets left Winnipeg for Phoenix. Peter Pocklington, owner of the Edmonton team that was once a hockey dynasty, has threatened since the early 1990s to sell the Oilers. Some Canadian fans of the sport turned to junior hockey, finding there the excitement the NHL once generated.

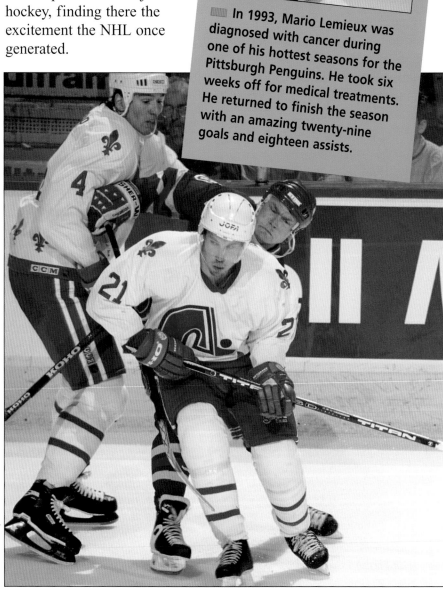

RECOVERY

In 1993, Mario Lemieux was diagnosed with cancer during one of his hottest seasons for the Pittsburgh Penguins. He took six weeks off for medical treatments. He returned to finish the season with an amazing twenty-nine goals and eighteen assists.

RETIREMENT

Wayne Gretzky played his final game in Canada on April 15, 1999, against the Ottawa Senators. He played the final game of his career three days later, against the Pittsburgh Penguins. After twenty years, the greatest hockey player in history retired from the National Hockey League. Fans across the country mourned Gretzky's retirement.

At the end of the 1990s, about 60 percent of NHL players were Canadian. But with a 182-percent increase in the number of Americans playing ice hockey since the beginning of the decade, Canadian domination of the sport was on the decline.

1972 – GOALIE

Manon Rheaume

Manon Rheaume began tending goal at age seven in Quebec's Atom league. When she cried after getting hurt during a hockey game one day, her father told her, "Macrame isn't painful. Choose!" Rheaume chose and returned to goal.

Years later, twenty-year-old Rheaume made hockey history as the first woman to play in an NHL game. Two years after the exhibition game for the Tampa Bay Lightning, she signed a contract with the Las Vegas

Thunder, part of the International Hockey League. While few doubted her skill, her small size sometimes held her back from more success in the men's leagues. Critics said that a woman may one day play in the NHL, but it will be a 160-pound woman, not a 120-pound woman. Criticism did not stop Rheaume, who said, " I don't get up every morning to practice just to be the first woman to play hockey. I really like the game."

▥ Since 1993, the number of women playing hockey in North America has increased by 308 percent.

Trans-Canada Trail

Not everyone has to be a professional athlete to enjoy sports in Canada. The Trans-Canada Trail was announced in 1994 as a millennium project. When completed, the 15,000-kilometre trail links every province and territory. Canadians will be able to walk, cycle, horseback ride, cross-country ski, and snowmobile across the country on the network of recreational trails.

With the help of a few corporations, the trail is built and funded by volunteers. Canadians may donate money in return for having their names inscribed on plaques along the path. John Bellini, executive director of the organization building the trail, says Canadians can celebrate Canada Day 2000 by hitting the trail. He says the project is a "perfect fit for the core values of Canadians, the things they have come to care about—clean air, fitness, doing safe and healthy things with their families, and getting back to nature."

●●●●● The Trans-Canada Trail

BASEBALL

▥ On October 24, 1992, the Toronto Blue Jays became the first team outside the United States to win the World Series. They defeated the Atlanta Braves. Joe Carter's series-winning home run is one of the team's most memorable moments. The Blue Jays came back in 1993 to win the series against the Philadelphia Phillies.

Gold Fever

It was a modern-day gold rush. Except this time people did not grab a gold pan and head for the hills. They phoned their stockbrokers and asked to invest in Bre-X Minerals. Bre-X was a Calgary company that claimed to have found a huge gold field in Indonesia in 1993. The amount of gold they claimed they found would have made it the largest gold find in the world.

Thousands of people rushed to invest in the company. Many people became rich just by selling their stocks to other people. In 1996, the fever for gold ended. The geologist who made the first gold claims died mysteriously when he fell from a helicopter. Then a company that was partnered with Bre-X announced that there was no gold at all. Bre-X went broke within days, leaving behind only mystery and scandal.

■ **David Walsh was the man responsible for selling Bre-X stocks. People still do not know whether he knew all along that there was no gold at the site.**

■ **In January 1990, $1.17 Canadian could buy $1.00 U.S.**

By January 1999, it took $1.52 Canadian to buy $1.00 U.S.

A Wealthy Barber

Next to the Bible, David Chilton's *The Wealthy Barber* is the best-selling book in Canadian history. The book tells the story of a barber and how he saves money. It teaches Canadians how to prepare for retirement.

The book's main idea is to save just a small amount of money every month. The money should be invested in a Registered Retirement Savings Plan (RRSP). RRSPs pay **interest** regularly, so the money grows. Over time, the barber argues, even ordinary Canadians can become wealthy.

"Probably the most important message I give is this: Start saving NOW!"

David Chilton

Days of Action

Ontario unions flexed their muscles in the fall of 1997. The Ontario Federation of Labour represented 650,000 **unionized** workers across the province. They organized a series of protests called Days of Action. Over a two-year period, nine city-wide **strikes** were held across the province. The Days of Action protested the provincial government's welfare and job cuts. The cutbacks were part of a program called the Common Sense Revolution. The "revolution" promised to reduce income tax and cut government spending.

One demonstration in London, Ontario, drew 20,000 people. Another in Hamilton attracted 25,000 people. The walkout by 126,000 Ontario teachers was the longest illegal strike since the end of World War II. The teachers had enormous support. Parents and students joined striking teachers on the picket lines. Although the teachers went back to work without getting their demands, unions said public support made the protest a success.

▬ **Thousands of people on strike brought Toronto to a standstill.**

Minimum Wage

In 1998, Alberta changed a law that had allowed companies to pay students under eighteen years old less than the minimum wage. Before the change, employers could pay students $4.50 per hour rather than the adult minimum wage of $5.00 per hour. Alberta also raised its minimum wage to $5.90 by the end of 1999. Ontario and the Northwest Territories continued to have laws that allowed employers to pay students a lower minimum wage than adults.

Minimum Wage	
British Columbia	$7.15
Alberta	$5.90
Saskatchewan	$5.60
Manitoba	$5.40
Ontario	$6.85 ($6.40 for students)
Quebec	$6.80
New Brunswick	$5.50
Nova Scotia	$5.50
Prince Edward Island	$5.40
Newfoundland	$5.25
Northwest Territories	$6.50 ($6.00 for students)
Yukon	$6.86

Balancing Budgets

Governments across Canada worked through the 1990s to balance their budgets. This meant they wanted to spend no more money than they took in through taxes. Businesspeople liked this trend because it made governments operate more like businesses. Balanced government budgets encourage businesspeople to invest money and make their businesses grow. This helps the economy grow by employing more people.

Not everyone saw the balanced budgets as a good thing. Budgets are balanced by either spending less money or making more money. In most cases, governments chose to spend less money. Some people argued that this was the wrong choice. Cutbacks meant unemployed people no longer received as much money to live from programs such as welfare and Employment Insurance. In other cases, people paid the same or more money for less service. Many people were angry about decreases in health care because of cutbacks. Critics of spending cuts argued that governments should balance their budgets by taxing wealthy people more, not by spending less.

Olympic Roots

When Roots Canada won a contract to supply uniforms to Canada's Olympic athletes, it seemed like a good agreement for everyone. Roots made casual clothes that were comfortable, attractive, and popular. Each athlete on Canada's 1998 Olympic team received five sets of free clothes. In return, Roots was able to sell copies of the same clothes in their stores.

Roots and the Canadian Olympic Association both made a lot of money from the deal. The only people not happy were some of the athletes. Seeing their Olympic uniforms for sale everywhere made their Olympic experience seem less special. Rower Marnie McBean explained that most Olympic athletes, "don't win a medal, don't get sponsors. The only thing they have is the sense that they're part of something, wearing the Canadian uniform—when you devalue that, you take away the only thing they have."

■ Figure skater Elvis Stojko and biathlete Myriam Bedard enjoyed their Roots clothing at the 1998 Olympics in Nagano, Japan.

Hip-hop

Inspired by rap musicians, the hip-hop look lasted throughout the nineties. Extra-large blue jeans that looked "phat," baseball caps, hooded sweatshirts, and baggy shorts made the hip-hop look. Topped off with a jacket with a sports team logo, the look was complete.

Crisp and Comfy

What did the popularity of snowboarding do for fashion? It had hundreds of young people wearing clothes made for movement. As one teen noted, "I buy whatever I like, as long as it's comfortable and looks good." Baggy pants with big side pockets, loose jackets, and roomy plaid shirts allowed boarders to perform "airs" in the snow or on the streets. Ski toques, shockproof watches, and cool sunglasses completed a "crisp" boarder outfit.

FADS

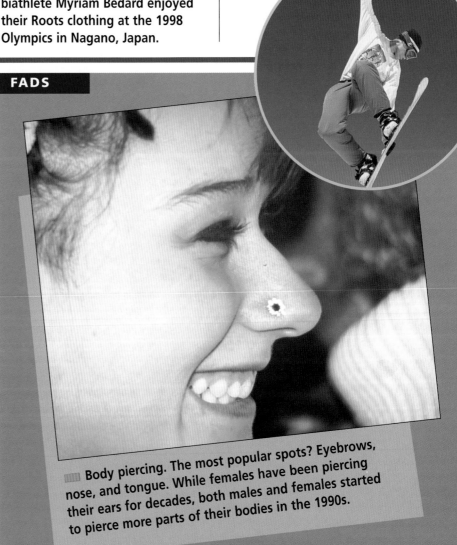

■ Body piercing. The most popular spots? Eyebrows, nose, and tongue. While females have been piercing their ears for decades, both males and females started to pierce more parts of their bodies in the 1990s.

Rise and Fall of the Supermodel

For most of the 1990s, the fashion world loved six women known as the supermodels: Christy Turlington, Naomi Campbell, Cindy Crawford, Claudia Schiffer, Kate Moss, and

Supermodels are no longer the only faces we see on magazine covers.

Canadian Linda Evangelista. They were international stars. Their faces were on the covers of every magazine, even those usually reserved for movie stars.

By the end of the decade, "the look" had shifted. Glamour returned to Hollywood. Magazines wanted stars, not models for their covers. Actors such as Julia Roberts and Gwyneth Paltrow were the centre of attention. Magazine fashion spreads also showed women with quirky, less-than-perfect looks. Fashion experts explained that a change to less flashy clothes required models who did not overpower the new looks.

From Grunge to Glamour

The early nineties look was "grunge." Alternative rock groups such as Nirvana made it fashionable to be comfortable. The look involved layers of thrift shop clothes, baggy, torn jeans, and large flannel shirts. Grunge rockers spent time "moshing" to hard rock bands.

By the end of the decade, grunge was out. Trendsetters wanted glamour. Gloves, satin, suits, and cocktail dresses were the new looks. Bands playing jazz and swing music from the 1920s and 1930s were in. Hip crowds danced the jitterbug and made going out an event worth dressing up for.

"People are sick of rock clubs and ripped jeans.... They want elegance."

Nils Bernstein, musician

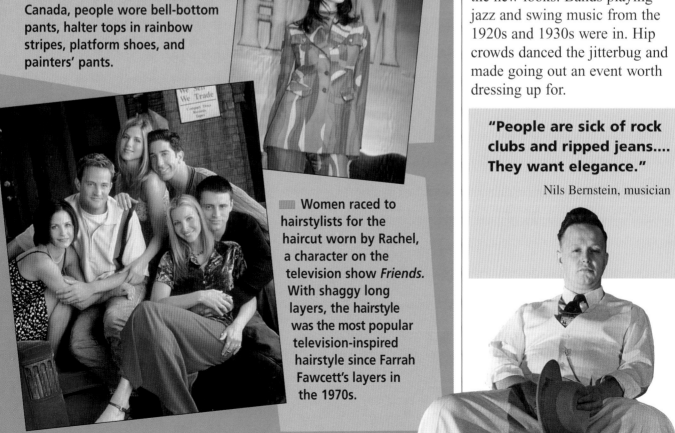

By the end of the nineties, the seventies were back. All over Canada, people wore bell-bottom pants, halter tops in rainbow stripes, platform shoes, and painters' pants.

Women raced to hairstylists for the haircut worn by Rachel, a character on the television show *Friends*. With shaggy long layers, the hairstyle was the most popular television-inspired hairstyle since Farrah Fawcett's layers in the 1970s.

Census Years

The census is an official count of the population by the Canadian government. A census gathers information on a wide variety of matters, including immigration. Two census tallies were held in the 1990s: in 1991 and in 1996. The map shows the percentage of Canada's immigrants who came from different parts of the world during these years.

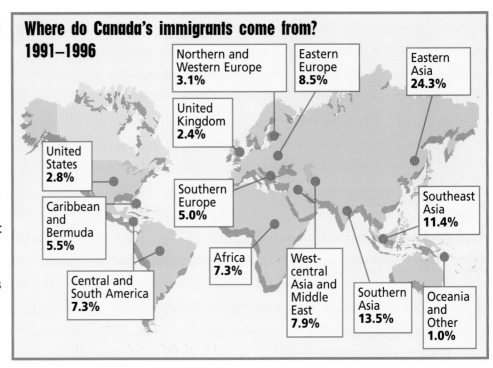

Where do Canada's immigrants come from? 1991–1996

Northern and Western Europe **3.1%**

Eastern Europe **8.5%**

Eastern Asia **24.3%**

United Kingdom **2.4%**

United States **2.8%**

Caribbean and Bermuda **5.5%**

Southern Europe **5.0%**

Southeast Asia **11.4%**

Central and South America **7.3%**

Africa **7.3%**

West-central Asia and Middle East **7.9%**

Southern Asia **13.5%**

Oceania and Other **1.0%**

Comparing the Canadian Immigrant

How do immigrants compare with people born in Canada? One way governments can tell how well immigrants adapt to life in Canada is to compare them to people who are born in Canada. Take the following quiz to see how much you know about Canada's immigrants. All answers are based on the 1991 census.

Are Canadian immigrants more likely, less likely, or about as likely as people born in Canada to ...

1. have a university degree?
2. have less than a Grade 9 education?
3. be employed?
4. own their own business?
5. have a full-time, full-year job (not seasonal or part-time work)?
6. live in a major city?
7. be over the age of sixty-five?

Answers:

1. More likely. 14% of immigrants aged fifteen and over have a university degree, compared to 11% of people born in Canada.
2. More likely. 19% of immigrants have less than a Grade 9 education, compared to 13% of the Canadian-born population.
3. As likely.
4. More likely. 16% of employed immigrant men are self-employed, compared with 12% of Canadian-born men. 8% of immigrant women are self-employed, compared to 6% of

Canadian-born women.
5. More likely. 63% of employed immigrant men have full-time, full-year jobs, compared to 59% of Canadian-born men. 50% of employed immigrant women are fully employed, compared to 45% of Canadian-born women.
6. More likely. 84% of all immigrants live in a major city, compared to 56% of the Canadian-born population.
7. More likely. 18% of immigrants are over sixty-five years of age, compared to 10% of people born in Canada.

Immigration and the Economy

Immigration patterns affect local economies. During the 1990s, hundreds of Asian immigrants settled in Vancouver. They bought houses and built large apartment and office buildings. Vancouver real estate prices rose because many of the immigrants were wealthy and could afford to pay high prices. Vancouver homes became some of the most expensive to buy in North America.

In the late 1990s, many immigrants returned to their countries in Asia. In the first nine months of 1997, 6,000 people left Vancouver to return to Hong Kong. Many homes were for sale, so people buying homes had more choice. This meant prices dropped suddenly. People who bought homes in 1996 for $500,000 might be able to sell them for only about $400,000 in 1998.

COMING TO CANADA

▓ Canada is one of the few countries in the world with an active program for permanent immigration. In fact, Canada accepts more immigrants and refugees, in proportion to its population, than any other country.

One out of every six Canadian residents was born outside the country. Directly or indirectly, immigration policy has touched the lives of every Canadian, and it has helped to make Canada a culturally rich, prosperous, and progressive nation.

Excerpt from the Conicor Consul International Group web site at
http://www.conicor.ca

The Future of Immigration

What makes information about Canada's immigration policies unusual? It is offered through the Internet on the World Wide Web. Conicor is a company that helps prospective immigrants apply to live in Canada. Their web site offers people a fast and easy way to get information about Canada and Canadian immigration rules.

A web site for immigration information makes sense if you think about the kinds of immigrants accepted in Canada. New immigrants are grouped in three classes. Economic class immigrants are businesspeople and skilled workers. Family class immigrants are usually relatives of people already living in Canada. Humanitarian class immigrants are people escaping war or other poor conditions in their home country. In 1996, 55.5 percent of new immigrants were from the economic class, 31.3 percent from the family class, and 13.2 percent from the humanitarian class. This means more than half of the immigrants to Canada are likely to be educated businesspeople or workers with computer skills.

The State of Multiculturalism

"It just seems very natural. It's not something that we think about—it's just the way it is," said one Canadian about multiculturalism. Canada is a multicultural country, which means Canada is made up of many different cultures. Multiculturalism is especially common in cities. In 1998, 42 percent of Toronto's residents were born outside Canada. The average across the country is 17 percent.

Many people believe having different cultures is good because people can learn from one another. However, differences can also cause barriers. Critics of multiculturalism believe Canadians are kept divided because they keep within their own cultural heritage. On a street in Toronto that has families from many cultural backgrounds, one young man said his neighbours do not really know each other, "Everybody's on a 'hi, bye' basis."

"[Multiculturalism gives children] a sense of what goes on in the real world. Life isn't just their own little community.... Difference isn't bad, it enriches your life."

Marisa Morelli on raising her children in a multicultural neighbourhood

▓ An average of 220,000 immigrants arrived in Canada each year in the 1990s. Most new immigrants became Canadian citizens.

Music

1965 –

Shania Twain

You would never guess it from her glamorous videos, but Shania Twain is no stranger to hard times. Her family did not have much money as she grew up. She started singing in country bars when she was eight years old to help her family survive. When she was in her early twenties, her parents were killed in a car accident. She continued singing to support her younger siblings. She changed her name from Eileen to *Shania*, which means "I'm on my way" in Ojibwa. Shania wanted to honour her adopted father, an Ojibwa man. "I took [Shania] because I wanted something unique and something beautiful for myself and also, since my dad wasn't alive anymore, I felt it would somehow keep me connected to him."

She recorded an album in 1993, but it was not very successful. For her second album in 1995, Shania and her husband wrote the music. *The Woman in Me* became the world's best-selling album by a female country music artist.

> "Most people's growth is done in private; an artist's growth is done in public. I thank Canada for accepting that in me."
>
> Alanis Morissette at the 1996 Juno Awards

1974 –

Alanis Morissette

Pop star Madonna said Alanis Morissette reminded her of herself when she was starting her career. In 1995, Madonna saw a tape of Alanis performing. Madonna's recording company jumped at the chance to sign the young singer to a contract. The result was *Jagged Little Pill,* a smash hit in 1995. Alanis became the first female Canadian with an album at the number one position on *Billboard*'s top 200 album chart.

Her music was praised for being full of emotional truth. For many people in the music business, her music was a surprise. In 1992, while still in high school, Alanis recorded an album that was a pop hit. Critics disliked her dance-style music and did not take her talent seriously. When Alanis's second album flopped, even with fans, she took time off for several years. With her 1995 comeback, she gained the respect of both fans and critics.

1968 –

Céline Dion

The youngest child of fourteen, Céline Dion started singing and performing with her family when she was just a child. She met her manager René Angélil in 1981 when she was thirteen years old. That year her career took off. She quit school and went on tour with her mother and René. "I missed my family and my home, but I don't regret having lost my adolescence. I had one dream: I wanted to be a singer," Céline said.

Her dream came true. She has recorded albums for both English and French audiences, and she has had record-setting hits for both. In 1994, her wedding to

> "I don't want to sell 5 million records and be rich, and then that's it. I'm afraid of that. I want a career. I want to sing all my life."
>
> Céline Dion

René was one of Montreal's biggest events. Traffic in the city was blocked for four hours as fans and media tried to catch a glimpse of the newlyweds.

In 1999, Céline was awarded four Juno Awards and three Grammy Awards. Two of the awards were for best pop female vocalist and best francophone album.

Barenaked Ladies

Some bands might be surprised if audience members threw macaroni on stage. But not the Barenaked Ladies. For band members Steven Page, Ed Robertson, Tyler Stewart, Kevin Hearn, and Jim Creegan, it was all part of a night's entertainment. Ed Robertson explained that "We are geared to giving people a good time. We approach [performances] as an ongoing conversation with our audience." The pasta-throwing crowd was responding to one of the band's

hits, "If I Had $1,000,000," in which band members praise Kraft Dinner.

The Barenaked Ladies have a wacky, fun style of music and performing. Fans love their humour. The band's fifth album, *Stunt*, has sold nearly 4 million copies.

1968 –

Sarah McLachlan

"I wanted my independence like everyone else that age, and I guess I was luckier than most to have it offered to me on a platter," explained Sarah McLachlan about her quick success. She was offered a recording contract when she was just seventeen, but her parents would not let her accept it. When she was nineteen, another offer came and Sarah moved from Halifax to Vancouver to begin her career.

She became famous for more than her respected albums in 1996. When Sarah requested that another female performer open her concert, she was told it was impossible. Concert promoters said audiences would not accept

an all-woman act. The refusal brought out Sarah's rebellion, "I wanted to prove them wrong—and so I did." The result was Lilith Fair, a touring festival of female acts that became one of the biggest, most popular tours of 1997. Lilith Fair toured to great success again in 1998 and 1999.

East Coast Music

East Coast musicians dominated much of the Canadian music scene in the 1990s. Part of this domination may be because there is so much music on the East Coast. People explain that making music is an important part of East Coast culture. Audiences are not supposed to just sit and watch a musical act. Talented or not, they are supposed to participate. Children grow up making and creating music.

This culture turned out a string of national and international successes during the 1990s. Fiddlers such as Ashley MacIsaac and Natalie MacMaster gave traditional sounds their own twist. Bands such as the Rankin Family, Irish Descendants, and Great Big Sea had hits with both traditional and original music. Many of these hits deal with issues common in East Coast life, like the closing of fisheries and unemployment. So many bands were on the scene that the East Coast Music Awards was regarded as the place to hear some of Canada's best music.

■ Ashley MacIsaac was a leader in the East Coast music scene during the nineties.

Douglas Coupland

Douglas Coupland's 1991 novel *Generation X: Tales for an Accelerated Culture* did not paint a bright future. The book was about the lives of people who were born from the late 1960s to the early 1970s. The main characteristic of Generation Xers was that they were born too late. People who were born from the end of World War II to the late 1960s—the Baby Boomers—had taken all the best jobs by the time the Xers entered the work force. By the time the Boomers retire, most Xers will be too old to take their place. Instead of careers, many Xers face "McJobs," work with low pay and little future. Coupland's novel helped many Boomers and Xers understand how the world is different for people who were born after the baby boom.

The Future of Generation X

lessness: a future of lower expectations than previous generations
from Generation X: Tales for an Accelerated Culture

"We basically walked out of school and into a permanent, full-time job. Companies were competing for us. The kids will never have it that easy."

Denise Stansfield, Baby Boomer

- Most Generation Xers do not expect to live independent lives until their late twenties or thirties. Many live at home on and off throughout their twenties.

- Most find job hunting difficult, even with family connections. Companies offer few rewards for loyalty, regularly hiring and laying people off. People frequently move back and forth between school and work as they move between jobs.

- In 1971, 32 percent of Canadians aged twenty to twenty-four were married. By 1991, only 8 percent of Canadians in this age group were married. By the end of the decade, the average age of marriage was twenty-eight.

- Over 70 percent of university graduates have jobs that have nothing to do with their education. Over 35 percent have jobs that require much less education than they have. But not getting a university education is not the answer. Since 1993, employment for people with only a high school education decreased by 28 percent.

▬ Because they could not find jobs after graduating from university, many Gen Xers went to foreign countries such as Japan to teach English as a second language.

"It's very different for us than it was for our parents. A lot of older people I talk to have a hard time understanding that it's not like when they were young."

Rob Anderson, Generation Xer

In the 1990s, each Canadian woman had an average of 1.6 children. To maintain the population at current levels, each woman has to have 2.2 children. Other industrialized countries face the same declining birth rate. Japanese women have only 1.5 children and Italian women 1.2. Neither of these countries accept many immigrants, so their populations will decline steadily.

Turning Grey

Canada's population is greying. This means the average age of Canadians is getting older. This trend grew throughout the 1990s and probably will not slow down for another two or three decades. As the existing population grows older and dies, a new population is not growing fast enough to take their place. In 1997, Statistics Canada reported that Canada's birth rate went down for the sixth year in a row. By the year 2020, Canada's rate of growth from new births will be 0 percent. In 1991, 11.6 percent of the population was over the age of sixty-five. By 2030, it will be 23 percent.

Why does a greying population matter? Most older people retire from their jobs and rely on savings and government pensions to live. Older people also tend to use the health care system more often. Government programs and health care are paid for with tax money. If there are fewer young people to pay taxes, who will pay for the programs? One answer is to increase immigration. At the end of the decade, Canada accepted about 1 percent of its population in new immigrants each year. By the year 2020, Canada may have to double or triple this number just to keep its population at the same level.

Decline of the Family

When you say the word "family," many people picture the traditional family: a mother, a father, and two or three children. Yet at the end of the nineties, this family was quickly disappearing. One-third of marriages ended in divorce, breaking up the family unit. Many children grew up with one parent, or a remarried parent and stepparent. Both parents often worked outside the home, so children spent more time with babysitters and at daycares.

Traditional communities were also disappearing. More people travelled to work outside the area where they lived and many worked longer hours. This meant fewer people got to know their neighbours. Many people even moved across the country or world to find better jobs. Family and friends were just as likely to E-mail each other to keep in touch as get together or even talk on the telephone.

Without strong ties of home town or family, people turned to their co-workers for support and friendship. Popular television shows such as *Ally McBeal* reflected this trend. Characters on the show behaved almost like a family. They argued, spent time outside of work together, and supported one another through hard times. Some companies encouraged this trend by getting pool tables and opening "coffee shops" in their offices. They saw these changes as the best way to keep talented, young employees.

Pacific Salmon

When the Pacific Salmon Treaty between Canada and the United States ended in 1993, it began a war of words. The treaty had required that fishers from each country catch only the number of fish that spawned in their own country's water. After the treaty ended, Canadian fishers claimed that the Americans were catching many more fish than their share. Fishers protested by blocking important water routes near Vancouver with their boats.

Discussions for a new treaty did not go well. At one point, Canadian **negotiators** called an end to the

There were other animals, such as bears, affected by the decrease in salmon stocks.

talks. Tension grew when British Columbia Premier Glen Clark got involved. Clark announced that he would cancel a U.S. navy lease to an area off Vancouver Island. Federal politicians on both sides of the border stepped in to help talks begin again.

CanCon

What is CanCon? A Mexican holiday resort? A French cabaret dance? CanCon stands for Canadian content, which all radio stations in Canada must provide. The Canadian Radio-television and Telecommunications Commission (CRTC) is a federal government organization. It regulates how much Canadian music you hear on the radio. The CRTC wants to give Canadian musicians a chance to compete against American artists. In 1998, the CRTC raised levels of CanCon from 25 percent to 35 percent. This means that from 6 A.M. to 6 P.M. on weekdays, at least 35 percent of the music played by radio stations must be Canadian. Canadian music is defined by the CRTC as music written or performed by a Canadian, or music recorded in Canada.

Many people objected to the change. They argued that most stations would not play a greater variety of Canadian bands. They would just play the same bands more times.

Saving Canadian Magazines

Canadians like reading stories about Canada. They want to know about Canadian athletes, heroes, writers, actors, accomplishments, and events. Every month Canadians prove this. Canadian magazines sell better than American magazines, even though American magazines cover 80 percent of the space at newsstands.

But magazines depend on advertisements to stay in business. In 1997, the World Trade Organization ruled that Canadian tax laws were unfair to American magazine publishers. They said Canada would have to find another way to protect its magazine industry.

Canadian publishers worried they would go out of business without protection. Without extra taxes, American magazines could sell advertising cheaper than Canadian magazines. If this happened, Canadian publications might lose important **revenue** to the Americans. In 1998, the federal government solved the problem. They passed a law to stop foreign publishers from selling advertising services in Canada.

"It's not that we don't like our neighbours to the south. But just as you wouldn't expect your next-door neighbour to record your family's memories or trumpet your loved one's accomplishments, neither can Canadians rely on our American neighbours to reflect our experiences on the pages of their magazines. That's up to us."

Rona Maynard in *Chatelaine* magazine

The Royal Canadian Mickey Mouse Police

What does Mickey Mouse have to do with one of Canada's most famous symbols? In 1995, The Mounted Police Foundation contracted The Walt Disney Company Canada to market the RCMP image. Disney managed the Canadian manufacturers who were licensed to produce consumer goods using the RCMP image—no rights were transferred and no control was lost. Critics called the agreement a sellout of Canadian culture. Jokes about the RCMP being a "Mickey Mouse operation" were everywhere.

Three years later, the fuss died down and most critics were quiet. "The way it used to be, there were trinkets and treasures from all four corners of the world of varying quality. Now it's all high-quality, Canadian-made products: Now we get royalties," explained Staff Sgt. Ken Maclean. And the royalties are used for a good cause. Since the beginning of the agreement, hundreds of thousands of dollars have been invested in RCMP community programs. The programs help crime prevention, drug awareness, youth education, and senior citizen support.

Where did it happen?

Match each number with an event.

a) Red River flood
b) Ice storm
c) Potential earthquake site
d) SwissAir Flight 111 crash
e) Westray mine explosion
f) Nunavut
g) Hibernia drilling platform
h) Home of Nisga'a Nation
i) Oka stand-off
j) *Lonesome Dove* film site

Answers: **1. b; 2. d; 3. f; 4. h; 5. a; 6. c; 7. e; 8. g; 9. j; 10. i.**

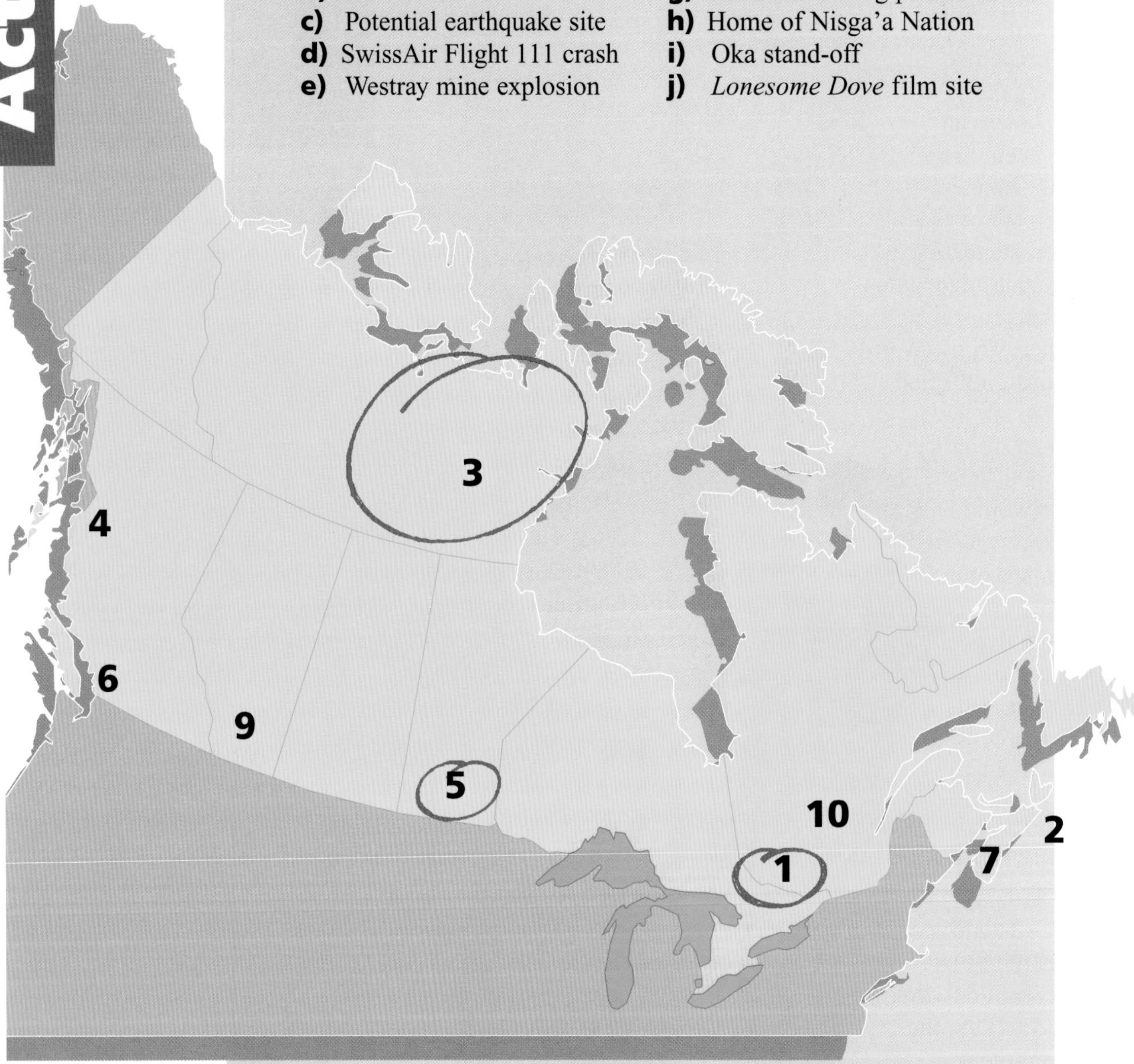

Trivia Challenge

Choose the correct definition for each word or phrase.

1. Greying

a) means that air pollution is causing polluted, greyish-looking snow in Canada

b) means that an increasing proportion of Canada's population is over the age of sixty-five

c) means that Canada is more than 125 years old as a country

2. The Wealthy Barber

a) a hair stylist from High River, Alberta, who won the lottery in 1994

b) a famous opera

c) a book about how Canadians should save money for their retirement

3. The English Patient

a) a survivor of the Ebola virus

b) a patient in Montreal who sued the Quebec government because he could not find a doctor who spoke English

c) a book about World War II

4. Lasagna

a) a Mohawk warrior involved in a stand-off with police

b) the food voted most popular in a nation-wide survey

c) what the Blue Jays ate for dinner the night before they won the World Series in 1992

5. The Millennium Bug

a) a flu virus that health officials worry will kill millions of Canadians

b) a computer problem that may cause serious disruptions around the world beginning January 1, 2000

c) a new car with a catchy advertising campaign

Answers: 1. b; 2. c; 3. c; 4. a; 5. b.

Newsmakers

Match the person or people in the news with their accomplishment. Watch out, there are more lettered answers than questions!

1. Held the longest illegal strike since the end of World War II

2. Father was a politician in Alberta for twenty-five years

3. First Canadian woman in space

4. Put up 7,000 crosses on the lawn of Parliament Hill to represent the number of people who will die from tainted blood

5. Race car driver

6. Asked Canadians to discuss their visions for Canadian unity shortly before the Citizens' Forum on National Unity gave its report

7. Won the first Olympic gold medal for snowboarding

8. Started female concert series

9. Quebec politician who has been a federal and provincial separatist

10. Has been called a "living cartoon"

a) Nova Scotia miners
b) Ontario teachers
c) Brian Mulroney
d) Roberta Bondar
e) Jacques Villeneuve
f) Kim Rowe
g) Jim Carrey
h) Ross Rebagliati
i) Preston Manning
j) Sarah McLachlan
k) Theodore Tugboat
l) Lucien Bouchard

Answers: 1. b; 2. i; 3. d; 4. f; 5. e; 6. c; 7. h; 8. j; 9. l, 10. g.

administration: the management of public affairs by government officials

allied: countries united by an agreement or treaty to support one another in times of war

apartheid: the legal separation of blacks from whites in South Africa

cartographer: a person skilled in making maps

compensate: to pay for or reimburse

contemporary: having to do with the present time; current

defiant: openly challenging or opposing

democratic: a system of government allowing citizens to freely vote their leaders into office

distortion: the act of pulling or twisting something out of shape and changing its appearance

economic: having to do with the production and distribution of wealth in a community or government

entombed: buried; shut in as if in a chamber for the dead

ethnic: a group of people with their own customs and beliefs

fictitious: made up; imaginary

Holocaust: the systematic killing of Jewish people by the Nazi forces from Germany during World War II

independence: freedom from any outside control

interest: money paid for the use of money

International Date Line: an imaginary line where each calendar day begins

investor: a person who uses his or her money to buy a part of a company or product that is expected to make money

Korean War: the first war during which world forces (including the U.N.) got involved to stop the fighting between North and South Korea

mock: make fun of by imitating

negotiator: a person who talks over problems in hopes of resolving them

Official Opposition: a political party that receives the second-most number of votes an election

prejudice: an opinion or judgment based on usually negative considerations

prime time: the period of time on television when the largest audience is expected, usually between 7:00 P.M. and 10:00 P.M.

quarantine: isolate

rat race: when daily life and work is exhausting and competitive

referendum: submitting a matter to vote

relinquish: give up; let go

revenue: income or source of income

revolution: a complete, and often violent, overthrow of a government or system

sovereignty: independence; freedom from any outside control

strike: refusal to work until certain demands are met

unionize: when a number of workers form a group to protect their interests in the workplace

Learning More

Here are some book resources and Internet links if you want to learn more about the people, places, and events that made headlines during the 1990s.

Books

Cameron, James and Randall Frakes. *Titanic*. New York: Harper Perennial, 1997.

Comish, Shaun. *The Westray Tragedy: A Miner's Story*. Nova Scotia: Fernwood, 1993.

Drake, Sylvie. *Cirque du Soleil*. Montreal: Productions du Cirque du Soleil, 1993.

Lowis, Peter. *South Africa, Free at Last*. Texas: Raintree Steck-Vaughn, 1996.

Tarcy, Brian. *Mario Lemieux*. Philadelphia: Chelsea House, 1998.

Webb, Michael. *Roberta Bondar: Leading Science into Space*. Mississauga, Ontario: Copp Clark Pitman, 1993.

Internet Links

www.aboutsnowboarding.com
This site reports all the news on snowboarding including celebrities, snow and resort reports, competitions, and their winners.

www.hibernia.ca/
This homepage contains information about the Hibernia project, the oilfield, and issues surrounding the project.

www.kermode.net/nisgaa
Created by the Nisga'a Tribal Council, this site details treaty news, the history and art of the Nisga'a Nation, as well as a directory of speeches, commentary, and book resources.

www.luco.gov.bc.ca/trancan/home2.htm
This B.C. TransCanada Trail site provides maps, photos, and related sites.

www.space.gc.ca
The Canadian Space Agency's bilingual homepage holds news releases, a careers page, the photo gallery, and their upcoming events page. There are also useful links and a "Kidspace" page.

There are many web sites where you can find information on people and events of the 1990s. Go to a search engine and type in key words to help get you started. For example, if you want to find out more about the ice storm, simply type in "ice storm."